the guide to owning a
Tarantula

Jerry G. Walls

T.F.H. Publications, Inc.
One TFH Plaza
Third and Union Avenues
Neptune City, NJ 07753

This book has been published with the intent to provide accurate and authoritative information in regard to the subject matter within. While every precaution has been taken in preparation of this book, the publisher and author assume no responsibility for errors or omissions. Neither is any liability assumed for damages resulting from the use of the information herein.

ISBN 0-7938-0383-7

Printed and bound in the United States of America

Printed and Distributed by T.F.H. Publications, Inc.
Neptune City, NJ

Contents

A male Cobalt Blue Tarantula, *Haplopelma lividum*, from Southeast Asia.

Ancient Spiders in a New Century

Almost 400 million years ago, before insects had developed flight, it seems likely that the spiders we today call tarantulas were already moving through the forests of the then strangely connected continents. If true tarantulas were not present, then their close ancestors certainly were around and the "true" tarantulas were soon to develop. There are few fossils of land animals from this period, and they are mostly fragmentary, but tarantula-like spinnerets and chelicerae (with fangs) have been discovered in rocks from New York.

RATHER TYPICAL SPIDERS

Though the tarantulas have an important place in the modern terrarium hobby, in many respects they are not especially unique spiders. Like other spiders, they have a body divided into two parts, the anterior prosoma and the posterior opisthosoma, connected by a narrow stem or pedicel that allows the digestive, nervous, and other organ systems to flow between the two parts. The prosoma is made of an upper (dorsal) carapace and a lower (ventral) sternum, both thickened, virtually seamless plates that support the legs and other appendages plus eyes and structures associated with the mouth and

A juvenile tree tarantula, *Avicularia versicolor*, looks much like a normal spider.

feeding. At the front end of carapace are the four pairs of eyes typical of most spiders, usually arranged in two symmetrical groups in a tight cluster. The carapace otherwise is almost featureless except for a middorsal groove that splits into a V shape distinguishing the anterior "head" from the posterior "thorax." Under the front end of the carapace is a pair of thick, often forward-pointing appendages, the chelicerae, each bearing at its tip a slender, slightly curved blackish fang with a tiny opening for the poison gland above its tip. In the tarantulas the poison glands are small and confined almost or entirely to the chelicerae, while in the more advanced spiders the glands are much larger and may occupy much of the space available in the prosoma. The poison glands are cylindrical sacs with narrow ducts leading to their openings in the fangs; thick muscles around the glands can quickly expel the venom, which serves mostly to immobilize prey.

Tarantulas (and all other spiders, for that matter) do not have true jaws as in more familiar animals, instead regurgitating digestive juices on the prey until its tissues become semiliquid and can be sucked into the tiny, permanently open mouth. Fine hairs and other structures around the mouth serve as filters so only the smallest particles actually enter the gut. Spines and tubercles at the bases of the chelicerae help break up the body of the prey, aided by large maxillae or endites, spiny plates at the bases of the pair of "false legs," the pedipalps.

The pedipalps look much like normal walking legs, and it is not difficult to incorrectly count five pairs of legs on some tarantulas. In addition to having maxillae developed at their bases, the pedipalps have one fewer segment than the true legs that follow them, lacking the metatarsus and thus having only two segments beyond the "knee" rather than three. In male spiders, including tarantulas, the tarsus or last segment of the pedipalp is modified to store sperm and transfer it to the female during mating.

All spiders have four pairs of walking legs that in tarantulas tend to be very similar in size, hairiness, and coloration (though the hind legs may be thicker in some species that are excellent diggers or jumpers). All arise from the sternum (as do the pedipalps) and consist of the following segments (given from sternum to tip): coxa, trochanter (very short),

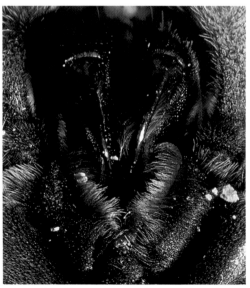

View of the fangs and mouthparts of a baboon spider, *Pterinochilus*.

6   THE GUIDE TO OWNING A TARANTULA

This male Usambara Orange Baboon Spider (*Pterinochilus* sp.) displays all the features of a typical tarantula, including the group of eyes at the front of the carapace and the pedipalps with one fewer segment than the legs.

femur, patella ("knee"), tibia, metatarsus, and tarsus. The tarsus ends in a pair of large claws with generally strongly toothed edges and usually large tufts of climbing and sensory hairs (scopulae). In some of the smaller tarantulas, but not the large tarantulas of the family Theraphosidae, there is a third small claw between the two large claws that, as in more advanced spiders, helps them handle silk.

There are numerous bristles, hairs, and spines on the legs of tarantulas and other spiders, these especially obvious and heavy in many common hobby species. Some sense the air and substrate for vibrations and air currents produced by prey and enemies, others record the chemistry of the substrate, while yet others end in microscopic triangular tips that allow a tarantula to climb relatively smooth surfaces, though not as well as in many smaller spiders. The number, development, and position of the various types of bristles and spines often are important in identification though difficult characters to use.

The opisthosoma comprises the globular abdomen plus its appendages, including the spinnerets near the tip of the abdomen. In some small tarantula families there are horny plates or rows of hairs on top of the abdomen, remnants of segments like those on the abdomen of an insect, but generally the abdomen of a tarantula is relatively featureless above except for variously developed hairs and other bristles. On the underside of the abdomen are a cliff-like ridge strongly developed in females and containing pockets for storing sperm (spermathecae), two pairs of book lungs or at least slits that represent their presence (in spiders book lungs are used for breathing), and two or three pairs of spinnerets (one pair often much longer than the others). The interior of the abdomen is occupied, as you would expect, by the various branches of the gut (which also extend into the prosoma), the primary reproductive organs (ovaries and testes), and the silk glands, plus the open circulatory system and ventral nerve cord.

In all these respects tarantulas are quite typical spiders, differing from more advanced spiders in the positioning of the fangs and the presence of two pairs of book lungs rather than one pair as in more advanced spiders. In these respects they are considered to be primitive, relatively little-modified spiders.

TARANTULA DIVERSITY

Every modern hobbyist knows what tarantulas look like: they are large, bulky spiders with many long bristles (hairs) on the abdomen and legs. They have large fangs at the ends of prominent chelicerae and do not spin flat, symmetrical webs. Unfortunately, this superficial description really applies only to the common species of one family of tarantulas, and the group is much more diverse.

Arachnologists, scientists who study spiders and their relatives (scorpions, solifugids, mites, etc.), currently recognize at least 15 families (and often several more) of tarantulas, comprising the arachnid suborder Mygalomorphae (formerly widely called Orthognatha) of the order Araneae (the spiders). Spiders today are thought to represent three major groups, the most primitive of which have the fangs flicking open forward and downward, more or less parallel to each other. Included here are the mygalomorphs plus a few even more primitive spiders that still show distinct segments on the abdomen (a few tarantulas show segmentation on top of the abdomen, though never strongly developed or continuous). The other spiders have the fangs positioned obliquely or perpendicularly to the ends of the chelicerae, thus opening under the chelicerae; these are the Labidognatha, the suborder that contains almost all the non-tarantula spiders living today, probably well over 32,000 species.

The 15 or more families of mygalomorphs are represented by at least 2000 described species, and likely almost as many undescribed, most of which are relatively small (under 1.5 inches, 3.7 cm, in body length), generally black or dark brown, and often glossy and nearly hairless. The small tarantulas, 14 families, form a complicated group that is enjoyed by arachnologists but largely ignored by hobbyists, though some make decent and interesting pets. Surprisingly, many of the small tarantulas are found in relatively cold regions, with a few, for instance, extending northward in the U.S. as far as Connecticut and Massachusetts.

The tarantulas of the terrarium hobby belong to the single family Theraphosidae, a largely tropical group with at least 800 described species that range from under an inch (2.5 cm) in body length—though rarely—to over 4 inches (10 cm) in length, with a legspan of up to 9 inches (22 cm). Though the family Theraphosidae is split into as many as 14 subfamilies by some scientists, largely on the basis of sexual characters, most of the tarantulas with a secure place in the hobby are found in only three subfamilies, the Theraphosinae (which contains most of the American terrestrial tarantulas), the Aviculariinae (including the common American tree-dwelling or arboreal species), and the Poecilotheriinae (stunningly patterned but dangerously venomous Indian arboreal tarantulas). Currently at least 100 species of theraphosids appear in the terrarium hobby at least occasionally, though perhaps over half of these could be considered suitable only for collectors

Major families of tarantulas
Mecicobothriidae
Microstigmatidae
Hexathelidae
Dipluridae
Nemesiidae
Barychelidae
Paratropididae
Theraphosidae
Atypidae
Antrodiaetidae
Cyrtauchenidae
Idiopidae
Ctenizidae
Actinopodidae
Migidae

with large pocketbooks rather than for hobbyists of average means.

AVAILABILITY

It is beginning to seem that the majority of tarantulas have rather small total ranges and occupy very narrow niches or microhabitats within their total ranges. Though there are many wide-ranging species recorded in the literature, as arachnologists look more closely at variation in such species as *Avicularia avicularia* (an arboreal species found over much of northern South America) and *Aphonopelma hentzi* (the common brown tarantula of the southwestern U.S.), they are finding that some variations are constant and have distinct geographic ranges and as such might be full species. Though there currently are over 800 species of true tarantulas (family

Purseweb tarantulas, *Atypus bicolor* (family Atypidae). Similar small tarantulas range north into New England.

Theraphosidae) described, it is probable that dozens or perhaps hundreds more exist and are still to be recognized by scientists.

Unfortunately, many of these undescribed species may never live long enough to be formally described. Because tarantula females live very long lives and seldom leave their burrows or family trees, it is easy to eradicate a species from a small area just as a side-effect of converting forest to grazing land or scrub to villages. Tarantulas are very dependent on moisture levels in their burrows, and their entire lives and physiologies are adapted to being sure they stay where the humidity is right. A tarantula may be able to go a year without catching a grasshopper, but it can only survive a few hours or days if its burrow is destroyed and no suitable habitat exists in which to rebuild it. Think how the soil in your garden reacts when you remove just a simple layer of mulch or dead leaves from the surface—the effects of sun and wind can dry out the top layers within hours, while even a normal rain can easily wash away loose soil. Just imagine what happens when a tarantula's habitat is logged over, removing the protecting trees, shrubs, and topsoil. It may simply be impossible to maintain a 75 to 80% humidity level no matter how deep a tarantula digs its burrow.

In addition to loss of habitat, tarantulas face other dangers to which they have not had time to adapt. One that is becoming important in the southwestern U.S. is loss of wandering males to traffic on desert highways. Males commonly only hunt for females for a few weeks each year, if weather conditions are right, and in some species males seem to be relatively uncommon. Every male crushed under the wheels of a car or truck or stomped under the heel of a camper removes a significant possibility of a female being fertilized and laying eggs. If the habitat is changed at the same time so the hatchlings cannot find a proper niche in which to develop, there is greatly reduced recruitment (i.e., young to replace dying adults) into a population over a period of years.

Over-collecting for both the terrarium hobby market and for biological specimens also has been important in determining the survival of tarantulas with restricted ranges. By the perversity of an open market, the fewer specimens of a tarantula exist in nature, the more likely that there is a cash market for that species. Tarantulas have been collected for biology classes and museum collections for years, and some species remain known only from preserved specimens collected a century ago. It is hard to tell whether the scientific market for preserved specimens has had much effect on tarantula numbers, but certainly in museums today there are very large samples, dozens or even hundreds of specimens, of a single species taken from a single locality over a short period of time. Such "authorized" or "validated" scientific collections certainly could put at risk a species with a narrow habitat and small range.

More likely to harm tarantula populations is collecting of adult females from their burrows for the hobby market. A female tarantula may live well over a decade and produce an egg sac with dozens to hundreds of young every year to three years, so each one removed from nature is a tremendous loss to the species. Commercial collectors have found that it is financially advantageous to locate colonies with large numbers of females, raid the burrows for as many females as can be found, and ship them all to American and European markets at a good profit. This is what happened in the early 1980's to the Mexican Red-knee Tarantula, *Brachypelma smithi,* from southwestern Mexico. Thousands of specimens, many or most adult females, left the country for Europe and the U.S. In 1985, the species was listed under CITES Appendix II, requiring that commercial exportations of specimens had to have permits both from Mexico and the destination country of each shipment. This allowed Mexico to strictly control collection and sale of *B. smithi,* and the country promptly placed an embargo on its exportation. Unfortunately, as late as the mid-1990's unscrupulous individuals still were collecting numbers of the species and illegally shipping them out of Mexico, but at least when shipments were intercepted the criminals were fined or even imprisoned.

The loss of wild-collected *B. smithi* from the terrarium market led to increased prices and a greater push for captive-breeding, with the result that Red-Knee Tarantulas are now less

Brachypelma smithi, the Mexican Red-knee Tarantula, long was the hobby standard but today is less available.

common and more expensive than 20 years ago but still are readily available to the serious hobbyist.

Restrictions on exports of Mexican Red-knees unfortunately caused dealers and hobbyists to shift their attention to other tropical American species as replacements, with the result that thousands of sometimes pretty tarantulas quite unsuited to the terrarium hobby were collected and sold from Mexican, Honduran, Costa Rican, Chilean, and other sources. Some of the replacement species had even more restricted ranges and precariously balanced populations than *B. smithi,* so the attempt to protect one tarantula species may have led to widespread endangerment of several other species. This problem was to some extent remedied when, in 1995, all species of *Brachypelma* were added to CITES Appendix II, resulting in fewer specimens of these colorful tarantulas reaching the market at higher prices.

It seems likely that further restrictions will be placed on commercial collecting of other tarantulas in several countries. For instance, at the moment there is a virtually uncontrolled flow of tarantulas from both eastern Africa and the Chinese-Vietnamese border area. Many of the species from these areas are large, aggressive, and possibly dangerously venomous. It also seems likely that they are being collected from a very limited number of colonies as many adult females are being shipped. China already has greatly restricted legal trade in its reptiles and amphibians, as has Kenya, and international scientific and conservation pressure is being brought to bear against other commercially important countries in these areas to limit shipment of all animals for the terrarium market. In the next few years tarantula enthusiasts will become more and more dependent on captive-breeding to supply their needs, which is best for both tarantulas and hobbyists.

A NOTE ON NAMES

The only real name that can be applied to a tarantula is its scientific name—a genus and species properly described by a scientist and validated or at least tolerated by other scientists. As in all animal hobbies, however, many enthusiasts, especially beginners, feel that it is too difficult to remember and pronounce scientific names, so they prefer to use common names in their own language. There is nothing wrong with this, though it makes communication more complicated as no rules apply to common names. Scientific names have to follow a rather complicated code of rules to be accepted, and though they are not perfect and there may be problems with some of them, they are recognizable internationally and from century to century. Common names vary from publication to publication, country to country, and even from year to year for the same species.

In this book I've chosen to follow what are relatively familiar common names for the species, based on usage in American, English, and French hobby literature. Specific common names (referring to a single species) are capitalized to prevent confusion with names for colors, thus the Red-leg will be said to have red legs. I am not attempting to follow any listing of "correct" common names promoted by any society or group. Remember that no rules control common names—they will be different in every language and, as long as they can be understood, any hobbyist is free to use any name he or she likes.

Scientific names are another matter entirely, as they are indeed controlled by rules that must be followed. However, at the moment the taxonomy—study of the identification and evolution of animals and plants—of tarantulas is in an incredible mess, and I can see no clear paths to follow through the morass of poorly defined genera and species. Some names—both newly proposed and older— are based on single specimens or on only one sex, and there have been little or no meaningful comparisons with previously described species. The differences between the genera of tarantulas often are small, so small as to question whether the genera are even distinct at all. For the purposes of this introductory book, I've chosen the course of least resistance and "gone with the flow"—I use the names that seem to be current in the hobby literature without attempting to determine whether they are correct or not. Expect that perhaps half the generic

New tarantula species, such as this *Brachypelma bicoloratum*, the Mexican Blood-leg Tarantula, constantly appear in the hobby.

names used in this book will change over the next 20 years and that a quarter of the species names represent either incorrectly applied names (i.e., the species in the hobby is not the one originally described under that name) or simple synonyms of correct names yet to be reworked from the hundreds of names in the older literature. Tarantula taxonomy is so inconsistent at the moment that no hobbyist should take the names too seriously—a very large grain of salt should be liberally applied to any taxonomic statement.

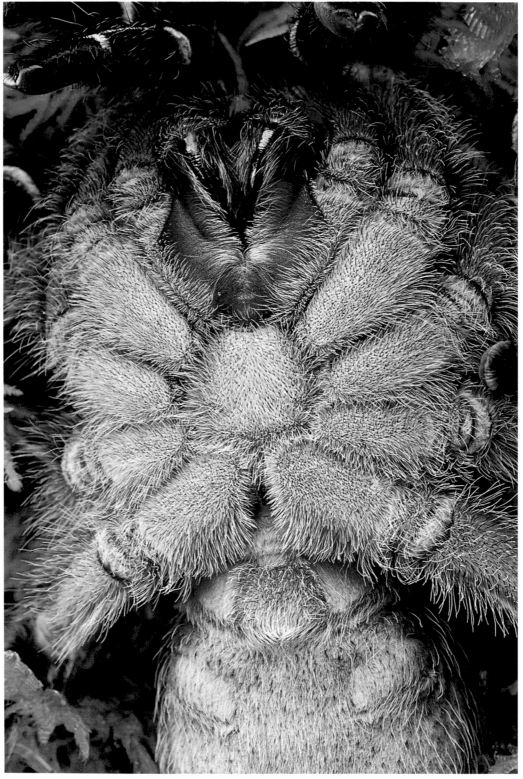

Ventral view of a Costa Rican Zebra, *Aphonopelma seemanni*, showing features of the cephalothorax and abdomen.

THE GUIDE TO OWNING A TARANTULA

Some Basic Biology

With few exceptions, tarantulas are nocturnal, very sedentary spiders that require relatively high humidity in a burrow, a tree web, or their general habitat in order to function. Their eight eyes see little in human terms, detecting mostly motion and, at perhaps distances under 8 inches (20 cm), shapes. They are "sit and wait" predators, spending hours each night sitting in or near the mouths of their burrows waiting for a suitable prey animal to pass close enough to grab as it goes by. Even the species that build large web nests in trees depend on happenstance for their prey. Tarantulas are not very intelligent even by spider standards and seem to have relatively few stylized behaviors of interest to biologists. Their major claims to biological fame are their large size (seldom under 1.5 inches, 3.7 cm, body length in theraphosids), general hairiness, and primitive characters such as two pairs of book lungs.

In captivity tarantulas follow their normal behavior patterns as much as possible—they spend the day under cover in a shallow or deep burrow or a thickly webbed perch near the top of the cage and at night come out to feed. Few tarantulas are voluntarily active

A male Costa Rican Red-leg, *Megaphobema mesomelas*, looks for a female at night.

during the day, and they do not appreciate bright lights. They like confined areas and even the tree-dwellers do not appreciate having their legs lifted off the safety of a firm substrate. Thus they do not like to be handled and often do not even like to be touched, rearing up on their hind legs, extending the pedipalps and front legs, and exposing the fangs in response to a perceived attack. All tarantulas will bite if forced to, and some will bite with little or no obvious cause. Aggressive tarantulas are infamous for attacking any movement, including drops of falling water and shadows of people passing in front of their cages, which makes some sense when you remember how poor is their eyesight. From this it should be obvious that it is never safe to handle any tarantula with your hands, never safe to place one by your face, and never safe to casually allow a tarantula to be placed where it could fall and damage the abdomen. The heart of a tarantula is a long tube down the center of the upper abdomen just below the soft skin; it is poorly protected from falls, and even minor damage could lead to internal bleeding and eventual death. In nature a tarantula taking a dangerous step, as when dropping from a perch even just a few body lengths, may spin a strand of silk that serves as a safety line. When you reach into a tank and pick it up, it has no safety line and is totally dependent on you for security.

HAIRINESS

Theraphosid tarantulas are among the most hairy of the spiders, with hundreds of hairs or bristles of various types covering the legs and body in set patterns that often are distinctive from genus to genus. The hairs serve many purposes, as you already know, from the long, delicate trichobothria that detect motion and touch to open-ended hairs that allow the pedipalps of a tarantula to determine the chemistry of a substrate, liquid, or prey. Special organs in the legs determine humidity levels, others seemingly record temperature, and still others react to currents of air as from the wings of a fly. Under the tarsi and sometimes metatarsi of tarantulas are large pads of small, specialized hairs, the scopulae, that aid the spider in climbing smooth surfaces and sometimes in digging. All the input from the many specialized hairs is analyzed by the brain (supraesophageal ganglion), located toward the front of the carapace.

Other hairs are purely defensive in function—bristles and spines make a

Notice the variety of hair types on this male Brazilian Salmon Pink Tarantula, *Lasiodora parahybana.*

The Haitian Brown, *Phormictopus cancerides*, is an aggressive species accused of having a dangerous bite.

tarantula a noxious mouthful for a predator. In many American tarantulas there are glassy hairs on the abdomen that are knocked off the abdomen when the spider is attacked, spines on the hairs embedding in the face and respiratory passages of a predator and causing it to back off. These urticating hairs will be discussed in a bit more detail later.

ARE TARANTULAS DANGEROUS?

I know that the standard answer to this question is, "Of course not. Their bite is no worse than a bee sting." However, this really is not true, and it is time hobbyists faced up to some facts. All tarantulas are venomous in the normal meaning of the word—all are very capable of voluntarily injecting a neurotoxic venom in an offensive or defensive bite. The Australian species of *Atrax*, a genus of the small tarantula family Dipluridae, are known to have killed at least a dozen humans, but they are not theraphosids so they really don't count. So what is there to worry about?

Actually, both ends of a tarantula can be dangerous to a hobbyist. You not only have to worry about the fangs and venom but also about noxious hairs kicked up from on top of the abdomen. The American tarantulas that tend to have weak venom and are fairly docile in captivity also tend to be the worst kickers. Though the venom of American tarantulas generally is innocuous, there are repeated reports of more than minor reactions to bites from some tropical

American species, especially in the genera *Theraphosa,* *Phormictopus,* and *Tapenauchenius,* all very aggressive tarantulas with which even a moment's lack of concentration could lead to a bite.

Tarantulas from Africa and Asia are even more of a potential problem to a hobbyist. The larger species from these areas tend to be very aggressive. Baboon spiders from eastern Africa have a nasty bite and also have allies (smaller species not yet in the hobby) that are known to cause human deaths in rare cases. The African arboreal tarantula *Stromatopelma calceatum* (occasionally imported for the hobby) has been reported to cause irregular heart beats after biting, and it is notorious for attacking rather than fleeing a potential enemy. Hobbyists often keep and breed the Indian and Sri Lankan ornamental tarantulas, *Poecilotheria,* noted for their bright coloration under the legs in many species. These colors may serve as warnings to predators that the spiders have a bad bite, much like the colors of a coral snake are thought to warn predators. Bites to humans have caused partial paralysis and affected heart contractions and blood flow, necessitating long hospital stays; a few deaths may have resulted from bites in the wild.

Unidentified tarantulas should never be handled and, like unidentified snakes and scorpions, probably should be considered dangerous until proved otherwise and treated as such. Be sure all cages are securely closed and locked, as well as being identified prominently as containing a dangerous animal. Do not handle the spider with the hands or tongs,

King Baboons, *Citharischius crawshayi*, are notoriously aggressive, move fast, and belong to a group that has caused human deaths.

THE GUIDE TO OWNING A TARANTULA

New imports from Southeast Asia, such as this female Cobalt Blue, *Haplopelma lividum*, often are dangerously aggressive and make poor pets for any but an experienced specialist.

but instead use a jar or bowl of the correct size and easily closable whenever moving the spider. Males often are more dangerous and aggressive than females, something to remember when evaluating the overall danger from a species of tarantula. Any tarantula bite that causes symptoms other than a few minutes of pain at the site of the bite should be submitted for medical treatment, though few doctors know anything about tarantula bites. Unfortunately, the major symptoms may occur many minutes or even a few hours after the bite, when the initial pain is long forgotten. Most side-effects of bites seem to respond well to treatment with bee-sting kits, but never take chances. You are dealing with a largely unknown field here, and you would not like to be the corpse given credit for being the first to die from the bite of a "harmless" tarantula.

MOLTING

Ecdysis, the shedding of the old outer skin layers, is a regular feature of tarantula life, allowing growth, replacing lost appendages, and generally refreshing the appearance. Adult female tarantulas commonly molt once per year, but exceptions are not uncommon. Spiderlings molt rapidly at first, then more slowly, with juveniles molting perhaps six times a year on average. When sexual maturity is reached, molting slows (females) or stops (males).

Tarantulas usually molt while lying on their back. They usually stop feeding a few days before molting, the abdomen may become very dark on top in pale-colored species, and the spider spins a thin, irregular web around itself as it lies in a humid, protected area. Molting may take one to six hours, with smaller spiders molting faster than larger ones, on average. During this time and the two or three days following molting a tarantula is very vulnerable and should not be touched. All food insects or other possible predators must be removed from the cage. Keep the light low, the humidity high, and just leave the spider alone.

As molting starts, fluid builds up between the old skin and a soft new skin (cuticle) that has formed below it. The fluid may cause the entire body to appear darker, as the old skin is slightly lifted above the new one over the entire body.

The first break in the old skin takes place above the bases of the chelicerae

The bald patch on the abdomen of this *Lasiodora klugi* (Bahia Scarlet) indicates a molt may be coming soon.

and proceeds along each side of the carapace until the entire carapace separates from the sternum as if it had been cut off with a can opener. The break continues from above the bases of the legs along the sides of the abdomen until the old abdomen is encircled by the slit. Both prosoma and abdomen separate readily from the old skin, which now is dry and wrinkled. The interior of the abdomen actually shrinks during molting as the blood is pumped forward into the carapace; the increased blood pressure there helps start the molt. As the carapace is popped free, the bases of the legs are pulled out of the old skin, often slowly and seemingly painfully, but most molts work out OK. To keep new joints soft, the tarantula often flexes the legs and chelicerae.

During a molt the tarantula sheds all parts of the body that are formed of cuticle, the tough skin of the spider. This includes not only the obvious surface of the body with all its spines, projections, fangs, etc., but many internal organ linings as well. Much of the lining of the gut is shed, as is the lining of the spermathecae in a female (which is why a mated female that sheds before laying is no longer fertile). Also shed are the coverings of the old fangs and the extremely delicate cuticle coverings of the tendons in the legs of the tarantula. Thus until the new cuticle hardens a tarantula cannot feed, fight, or flee. Chemicals in the cuticle react with the air to produce salts that gradually harden the skin, allowing the

A gorgeous *Brachypelma emilia*, the Painted Red-leg, lies next to its freshly shed skin. Notice its greatly increased size.

tarantula to return to normal functioning.

Because the shed skin of a tarantula retains virtually all the features of the living animal if properly preserved (usually by carefully spreading the skin and reattaching the carapace while the skin is still soft), it is useful for scientific work and may allow the identification of an unknown spider. All the hairs are retained in their normal position, as are the sexual organs. Specialists have discovered that the shed skins of immature female tarantulas, if examined closely, show traces of the spermathecae, the sperm storage pockets present only in that sex. By examining skins, it is thus possible to find out early in development (perhaps as soon as four to six months of age) if a specimen is a female or a male; males often are more desired by breeders because one male can fertilize several females during its short mature life. Unfortunately, telling sex from spermathecae in shed skins requires good optical equipment, comparison specimens, and lots of experience, so it is not useful to the average beginner. There are specialists who offer their sexing services for a small fee, however; they may be contacted through one of the tarantula societies.

LIFESPAN

Almost nothing is known about how long tarantulas live in nature. There have been few marking and recapture studies of these animals, where it is possible to trace an individual spider throughout its life from initial capture to death. It does seem that females of all normal-size tarantulas (perhaps 2 inches, 5 cm, body length and

Buying a captive-bred juvenile tarantula (such as this *Lasiodora parahybana*) assures you of an animal of known age and, regardless of sex, several years of having a good pet.

more) live long lives once they reach adulthood. Female lifespans of 15 to 20 years often are quoted, based mostly on records from captivity, with some *Brachypelma* supposedly reaching 30 years. Since a female terrestrial tarantula is exceptionally sedentary, seldom leaving her burrow by more than a few body lengths, she must live in very constant conditions and face few predators. If humidity is correct, molting seldom causes death; egg-laying does not seem to be dangerous; and few predators will tackle an adult tarantula in its burrow. If not dug out by a collector or forced out by deforestation, females face few challenges. Small tarantulas seem to live shorter lives, perhaps only 10 to 12 years, possibly because they develop faster. Large female tarantulas commonly take two to five years to reach maturity.

Males are another story. They are notoriously short-lived once they reach sexual maturity. They tend to mature sooner than females, often at only 18 months to three years, undergoing fewer juvenile molts. Their last molt produces the external sexual characters allowing it to transfer sperm to the female, and the rest of their life is spent hunting for females during what seem to be random trips into suitable habitat. After several successful matings their internal organs degenerate to some extent and they slowly die. Few male tarantulas live more than two years after maturity, and most die within a year of their sexual molt. Because they are more active, spending most nights exposed to predators and accidents, they also suffer a much higher mortality rate through "misadventure" than would females. In at least some

THE GUIDE TO OWNING A TARANTULA

Rarer species, such as *Megaphobema robustum*, the Colombian Giant, often are kept as single specimens with no intention of breeding. Only one sex may be available.

tarantulas the sex ratios are strongly skewed toward females, males being rare or at least rarely collected; captive-breedings also may rarely produce males in some species. In other species, however, at least in captivity, the sexes are equally represented. Because of the difficulties of collecting both sexes of many tarantulas, some species remain known from only one sex, often males collected accidentally while they crossed roads or ventured into houses.

A hobbyist who intends to keep a single tarantula of a species, with no intention of breeding, would be wise to start with a young adult female, preferably captive-bred. This way they will be sure to have a nice specimen for a decade or more. Unsexed immatures are always a risk to purchase if you do not intend to breed, as they may molt into males just as you get used to them, and then you are sure to lose your pet in just a few months.

The strange Brazilian Black & White Tarantula, *Braziliopelma* sp., is one of many poorly known species in the terrarium.

Rules of Care

Fortunately for hobbyists, the majority of available tarantulas can be kept quite simply with a minimum of fuss and bother. They need small cages with few decorations, a deep substrate into which to burrow if a terrestrial species or a group of branches on which to perch and web if arboreal, a small water bowl, and constant temperature and humidity conditions. Feeding is easy, as tarantulas have voracious appetites when in the mood to feed but can safely go months without eating. Captive-bred specimens of several common species are inexpensive, hardy, and colorful.

NUMBERS

There is only one thing to remember when keeping more than one tarantula in a cage—eventually you will have just one fatter tarantula in that cage. A few tarantulas are somewhat colonial in nature, with dozens or hundreds of females burrowing in a spot with good habitat or many arboreal adults and juveniles webbing over a few good snags and shrubs. In these cases each tarantula still has enough room to live its life

Tree tarantulas, here *Avicularia versicolor*, often are more delicate than terrestrial species.

without coming into contact with another tarantula, so fights are avoided. In the terrarium, there is little or no way to put two tarantulas in one cage and have them avoid each other. If the cage is large enough so each can have a corner and they are heavily fed, you may avoid disaster for weeks or months, but eventually there will be a misunderstanding and you will lose one specimen. Using a divider to partition a larger tank into smaller compartments will work, but only if the divider is firmly attached (tarantulas are strong and persistent), difficult to climb, and comes firmly into contact with the lid in such a way a tarantula can never move from one compartment to another—which is very difficult to assure. Why take chances? Always (except during short breeding intervals) house tarantulas individually.

CAGES

Tarantulas live with their backs against the wall; they are comfortable when their backs and sides are touching a firm surface. If you give a tarantula, especially a young, partially grown specimen, a roomy cage it will be nervous, find a corner, and disappear; it also may never be able to find any food. Give a tarantula a small terrarium that is proportionate to its overall legspan. Most common tarantulas are about 2 to 3 inches (5 to 7.5 cm) in body length and perhaps 4 to 6 inches (10 to 15 cm) in legspan, and for these a container no more than 12 inches (30 cm) long and wide and 8 to 12 inches

(20 to 30 cm) high is fine. Smaller tarantulas can be kept in smaller containers. Plastic and glass are excellent materials as they hold moisture; the top should be smooth (again glass or plastic) rather than screening as tarantulas will climb and show an unfortunate tendency to get their fangs stuck in fine screen mesh often used for tank lids, resulting in broken fangs (which may regenerate in one or two molts, just like a broken, cast off leg). Suitable cages include the smallest all-glass aquariums, "critter carriers" with the slotted lids replaced by a plastic sheet anchored along all edges, deep plastic storage boxes, plastic deli cups (for juveniles), even the plastic boxes sold to hold stuffed toys.

To ensure good air circulation, cut out 2-inch (5-cm) sections from opposing upper walls of a plastic cage and glue in micromesh, which contains thousands of nearly microscopic holes, or use a heated pin or tiny drill to puncture similar areas with very small (1/32 inch, 0.75 mm, or smaller) holes. A lack of air circulation could lead to the growth of fungus, making cleaning the terrarium more difficult.

Arboreal tarantulas need taller cages; allow at least 12 inches (30 cm) for a medium specimen. These tarantulas climb to the top of the cage and build a dense tube-web connecting the walls to their branches, and then they tend to stay there unless provoked to come down. Their cages often become very unsightly, but that's just the way it goes. Such a tall cage

Most terrestrial tarantulas can be kept in similar enclosures, though humidity requirements may vary. A Peruvian Black & Red, *Pamphobeteus* sp., may prove difficult to keep until its requirements are published.

preferably should open near the bottom to prevent rushes by the spider against your hand when you go in to feed and clean the cage.

SUBSTRATE

Arboreal tarantulas need little substrate, though there should be a layer of moisture-holding material of some type on the floor to help maintain the high humidity they need. In fact, it would not hurt to provide them with a deep substrate such as you would use for terrestrial burrowers, as humidity is if anything more important to arboreals than to terrestrials.

Never use gravel or sand as the base for the terrarium. These simply do not hold water. The best all-around substrate probably is about 4 inches (10 cm) of moist vermiculite. Vermiculite, an inorganic horticultural medium, is inexpensive and easy to find, and the dry, powdery substance holds a tremendous amount of water and releases it slowly. Take a quart (liter) or so of dry vermiculite and place it in a bucket, then add water to cover. When the water is all absorbed, add more; keep adding until no more water is absorbed (a day may be necessary for the process). Pour off the excess water and then by hand squeeze out the wet vermiculite until it holds together in your palm. Add enough of the moist mix to cover the entire bottom of the terrarium to the appropriate depth.

Mixtures of peat and sterilized potting soil also have been used as substrates, but they tend to dry out and harden quickly and often develop into mite cultures that may harm your spider. They do form an excellent burrowing medium, however, and some hobbyists prefer this mix to vermiculite. Many keepers compromise with a mix of all three substances. "High tech" tarantula terrariums have been constructed using the dense, soft plastic material florists use to form flower arrangements (not Styrofoam) and soft plastic-centered building blocks. Start the burrow where you want it and the spider will continue the job, lining it with silk just like a normal burrow.

Any substrate has to both allow a tarantula to burrow and hold sufficient moisture to assure a constant 70% or better humidity at the bottom of the burrow.

FURNISHINGS

Place a piece of curved natural cork bark or half a plastic flowerpot just off the center of the terrarium and loosely cover it with soil and mosses; the tarantula will do the rest. Remember that tarantulas like it dark, and they will cover exposed surfaces of the terrarium with webbing to reduce the light; a dark hidebox may reduce annoying webbing. A small water bowl, such as a bottle lid of appropriate size, should be sunk into the substrate; it must be shallow to prevent accidents. Some keepers place a few small pebbles or a wad of cotton wool in the bowl to make sure a small tarantula can not drown. If you wish, you can supply water in the form of a vial stoppered with a cotton plug and laid on its side; this will keep the tarantula from defecating in the water bowl.

Other furnishings are not necessary and may be harmful. Plants, real or plastic, will be dug up and displaced; rocks may slip and crush a tarantula, while driftwood and other branches have the same problem. Cacti are a no-no. All tarantulas will climb if given a branch, but this is not necessary for burrowers and it will just be covered with webbing. Never place any hard decoration near a wall where a climbing tarantula may drop on it and rupture its abdomen.

HUMIDITY

With few exceptions, all tarantulas do best with a burrow or tube-web humidity of 65 to 80%. Remember that this number refers to where the spider spends its day, not to the air in the terrarium. If the humidity drops below this level, the tarantula will slowly (or, in some cases, quickly) die. No exceptions. Just because a tarantula lives in the desert does not mean it is a dry-loving animal, as it burrows into a moist microhabitat. Arboreal tarantulas also live in a very moist world, using their dense webs to maintain humid conditions. They may desiccate even faster than burrowers.

If possible, purchase a simple, small hygrometer so you can have an accurate measure of humidity and place it as close as possible to where the tarantula prefers to spend its day, not just half-way up one wall as probably recommended by the manufacturer. An inexpensive electronic unit that measures humidity and temperature with a long probe is even better as you can place the probe right at burrow level.

Keep the substrate moist by adding water at the corners of the terrarium at regular intervals, keeping the cage in a water bath (which also helps prevent invasions of ants), keeping the water bowl topped up, and misting the entire cage once or twice a week. Never mist the tarantula directly; its sensory hairs react to water droplets as they would to contact with a potential predator, causing stress for the animal. Remember that arboreal tarantulas need somewhat higher and more constant moisture than terrestrial species and die faster if allowed to dry out.

HEAT

Almost all tarantulas are comfortable and grow well at 75F (24C), give or take 5 degrees F. Almost all will die if the temperature in the burrow or tube-web reaches 86F (30C) for any period of time. Lower temperatures, down to about 60F (16C), are tolerated well even for weeks at a time, though the spider will not feed and may become very sluggish. If in doubt or on vacation, err on the side of coolness, never heat. Remember that tarantulas occupy a microhabitat that may be very different in temperature from the surface exposed to sunlight. Since terrestrial tarantulas burrow down to escape the heat and dryness of the surface, you obviously cannot use undertank heaters for a tarantula, and hot rocks also are forbidden.

The best heating for a tarantula terrarium is room heating; keep their room warm enough so the burrow or tube-web stays at the appropriate temperature. If necessary, place a small space heater, especially one with a fan to help move the air, near the cage. Monitor terrarium temperatures carefully and continually, at the level at which the tarantula lives, not just at the surface. Also remember that warm environments allow a tarantula to lose water to the air faster than cooler ones, so at higher temperatures you will have to increase the humidity or at least keep a close eye on the hygrometer.

Other heating methods are preferred by keepers, but all have problems. Some place a heating strip or horticultural heating coil under one end of the terrarium, assuming the spider will never have to burrow on that side. Some use a 25- to 50-watt bulb suspended over the terrarium to provide fairly natural heat. Tarantulas tend to avoid light, but they cannot detect red, so a red bulb causes the fewest problems. The bulb can never be within the terrarium, as it will immediately be webbed-over by the spider, which surely will be burned; proximity to a light bulb also quickly leads to desiccation. Young tarantulas are especially subject to drying out. Ceramic heat emitters or black lights release no visible (to humans) light and can be used more easily than incandescent bulbs, but they may be too warm for most terrarium conditions. An old terrarium trick involving placing an aquarium heater in a jar of water will provide both warmth and humidity but is not reliable as the jar has to be constantly refilled or the heater will break; tarantulas will web over such makeshift heating jars, reducing their efficiency and possibly being burned in the process. Finally, an undertank heater panel can be mounted vertically against one wall of the terrarium, but you will find it difficult to produce a constant tank temperature with this method.

Any heater inside a terrarium produces problems and could lead to the death of the tarantula.

HANDLING

Basically, don't handle any tarantula. Any contact between your hands and the spider could easily result in injury to either or both of you. Never touch a tarantula with bare hands or even with gloves. They are quite delicate and easily crushed. The heart is at the upper surface of the abdomen and is not protected, so abdominal ruptures will lead to death. Use a pair of long forceps (tongs) or a flat stick to maneuver (NOT to pick up) a tarantula into a jar of appropriate size and then slide a piece of heavy cardboard over the top to transfer a tarantula from one cage to another. Remember that these spiders are very strong and will climb glass to lift off a piece of cardboard over the jar, even if it is "securely" weighted down. Never trust the tarantula to calmly stay in its jar for even a minute. Unfortunately, almost everyone does pick up pet tarantulas by hand. Grip them gently across the carapace, never by the legs, and try to support the abdomen.

Many African and Asian tarantulas react violently when a hand is placed in their vision. They stand erect on the hind legs, challenge with the front legs and pedipalps, and try to bite; they may even turn completely over onto their backs so the fangs can function from any direction. These tarantulas may be easy to cup with a jar directly from above, but remember that they may be very fast and also may jump several times their body length. Accidents often happen when a tarantula makes a wild, desperate jump toward an arm, runs up it, and then drops to the floor—and death. Along the way it may take several bites or spray irritating hairs in your face. Handle such tarantulas as little as possible and never take your eyes off them for even a second when the terrarium is open.

FEEDING

Crickets, from pinheads to adults, are the standard terrarium fare for most tarantulas from spiderlings to common adults. Crickets are bred in tremendous numbers, are available in many pet shops at low cost and in several sizes, and can be purchased all year long. They are clean, without pesticide residues or mites. Unfortunately they have little food value if just allowed to stay in a container without feeding for several days, so give them a diet of chopped vegetables or commercial cricket food while they are waiting to serve their purpose.

Spiderlings require tiny insects as food, usually pinhead crickets or flightless fruitflies. Tarantulas much over 4 inches (10 cm) in body length may take pinkie mice on occasion and certainly will take adult grasshoppers as well. Avoid feeding beetles, ants, wasps, stinkbugs, and other noxious or dangerous insects, as they may be able to hurt your pet. Additionally, chemosensory hairs on the pedipalps and front legs of tarantulas can quickly sense the chemicals secreted by stinkbugs and ants, and these foods will be rejected. Cockroaches, especially if captive-bred and thus not carrying pesticide residues, are an excellent food. The largest tarantulas, such as *Theraphosa blondi,* the Goliath Bird Eater, may be able to dispatch and eat adult mice, but mice also can kill and eat tarantulas.

Tarantulas generally require living prey or at least freshly killed food. All are carnivores; none take vegetable matter. A spider can tell fresh food from old food by touch; they also can orient to the movements of their prey through detecting vibrations in the substrate and fine currents in the air. Light is not necessary for a tarantula to feed, and they do best in near-dark conditions with very low light levels. Though some tarantulas stalk their prey, many just sit and wait for the cricket or fly to venture close enough to grab.

Spiderlings should be fed several times a week, but adults need to be fed only once a month to simulate natural conditions. In nature it is likely that prey seldom ventures into range of a tarantula, and feeding may occur only a few times a year. The prey is grabbed with the pedipalps and quickly bitten, injecting enough venom to instantly immobilize it. It then usually is crushed by the chelicerae and maxillae while being digested externally or may be covered with silk and held for later feeding. Webbing prey often happens when there is a sudden abundance of insects and the opportunity to get several morsels quickly. It may take an hour or more to ingest a cricket and about 6 to 12 hours to digest it and pass the dry crystalline wastes. Remember that a tarantula does not actually swallow its prey, instead reducing it to liquid outside the mouth; the hard parts of the food are formed into a dry pellet that is left behind when the spider is finished feeding. Pick up pellets and feces when you see them, before they fungus.

MAINTENANCE

Tarantula terrariums are more or less self-contained, and if you just remove old food regularly and keep the sides more or less clean, while keeping the water bowl clean and topped-up, you've done most of what is needed to keep the cage presentable. Many tarantulas, especially those from Africa and Asia, produce prodigious amounts of silk that may extend from their burrows to cover the water bowl, the surface of the substrate, all four walls of the tank, and even the lid. If you remove the webbing, the spider just adds more. Some of this behavior is to reduce light entering the terrarium during the day, but part of it must be some distortion of natural behaviors. Learn to live with the webs—they are just part of the fun of keeping a tarantula.

A mass of early instar Peruvian Giant Pink-toes, *Avicularia urticans*.

THE GUIDE TO OWNING A TARANTULA

Breeding and Spiderlings

When a wide variety of tarantulas was available cheaply just a few years ago, successfully keeping one or two tarantulas through their natural span of years was all most hobbyists really wanted to do. Most tarantulas were wild-collected adults or subadults of unknown age and often of uncertain species. Breeding was a rarity and sometimes more of a nuisance than blessing. The challenge of breeding was met by a relatively few dedicated hobbyists and commercial breeders, but there was little market for spiderlings, which were considered to be delicate and would not even look much like their parents for at least a year, sometimes more.

Much of this attitude changed when the most attractive and docile tarantulas (such as Mexican Red-knees) began to disappear from the market as wild-caught adults. This was due to countries such as Mexico imposing exportation restrictions, traditional commercial sources becoming unavailable due to politics, and decreasing numbers of some species in the wild. Captive-breeding now seems to be the only way that many tarantulas will survive in the hobby, and there are hundreds of breeders today, both hobbyist and small-scale commercial, producing captive-bred spiderlings of perhaps 50 species on a regular basis.

Many Mexican tarantulas, here *Brachypelma emilia*, are legally available only as spiderlings.

Because of their cannibalistic tendencies, all tarantula adults are kept separately, regardless of sex. This securely divided terrarium holds two *Avicularia versicolor*.

Many of the most successful breeders are in Europe, but quite a few breeding facilities have been developed in the U.S. as well.

Today any dedicated hobbyist can hope to breed at least one or two species and rear the spiderlings to adulthood. The process is slow and you will never receive immediate gratification, as mating to hatching may take almost a year and you will have to wait at least a year until you have a spider that even begins to look like its parents. Breeding requires dedication, patience, lots of small containers, and usually a continuous source of flightless fruitflies and pinhead crickets.

SEXES

Female tarantulas are as a rule somewhat larger than males, with heavier abdomens (capable of holding many eggs and more and larger silk glands), relatively shorter and often thicker-appearing legs, and always with simple pedipalps. Between the two pairs of book lungs is a raised platform, the uterus externus, sometimes miscalled the epigynum. (A true epigynum only occurs in more advanced spiders.) This marks the opening of the genital pore, the opening of the oviducts to the outside, plus a pair of blind sacs used for sperm storage, the spermathecae.

Spermathecae are found only in females, and they can be detected with magnification on the inside of shed skins of tarantulas just four to six months old. The abdomen of a shed skin is softened with warm soapy water and turned inside out. The two pairs of book lungs will appear as small whitish squares; the spermathecae will be located just to either side of the midline along the thickened slit of the uterus externus. The spermathecae sometimes are fused into a nearly continuous pocket, and at other times each sac is split, Y-shaped at the end. It takes a great deal of experience to consistently distinguish spermathecae in small tarantulas, and the task must be learned from an expert or through trial and error.

Males generally appear less bulky than females, with smaller abdomens and longer or more slender legs. Until their final molt when they attain adulthood, a male is difficult to distinguish from a female of the same age and size, but in his last molt he develops one and sometimes two secondary sexual characters that assure correct identification. The primary feature of a mature male is a sperm bulb growing out the underside of the tarsus (last segment) of each pedipalp. The sperm bulb usually is held rather close to the tarsus and may be covered by long hairs from the tarsus, but it should be easy to see if present. In addition, the scopula, the thick brush of adhesive hairs at the end of the tarsus in immature and female tarantulas, is absent or abnormally developed. The bulb ends in a simple, very fine tip that may be short or long, straight or twisted, but is open at the very end; this tip is the embolus, a type of pipette through which the sperm is drawn into the bulb and then passed into the spermathecae of the female.

A breeding pair of tarantulas (here *Avicularia versicolor*) may look like a mass of waving legs.

Additionally, in most male tarantulas there is a dark brown or blackish forked appendage, the tibial apophysis, that develops near the front end of the tibia (the leg segment after the patella or knee), usually on the inner, underside of the segment. The form of the apophysis may vary greatly in different genera of tarantulas and sometimes in different species of the same genus, so it often is used as a taxonomic character by arachnologists. Only a few tarantulas in the hobby (such as *Theraphosa blondi*) lack tibial apophyses.

TIMING

Males mature faster than females, usually undergoing their final molt when two or three years old. At this time the sperm bulb and tibial apophyses become visible and the tarantula may become obviously more nervous as hormones inducing it to look for a mate take over its behavior patterns. They may become very aggressive or more passive, depending on species and individual, but in either case their life is now rapidly ticking to an end. If not allowed to mate, a male may live another two to three years before dying; after mating the first time, he may live only six months to a year. Sperm is produced about two months after the molt, at which time the male is ready to be bred.

Females mature more slowly than males, often taking three to five years to reach full size. As she approaches maturity she molts less often, until finally she molts only once a year. An adult female usually can be told by its large size and obvious uterus externus compared to immatures, but it is not always easy to tell young mature females from immatures. When the female molts into adulthood, she becomes matable, though usually she is not fully ready to accept a male for six to eight weeks after the molt. Barring accidents, she may live another 10 to 15 years, sometimes more, and be able to lay eggs every year to three years over this span.

MATING

Assuming you have an adult female that molted about two months ago and a male who had his adulthood molt two to six months ago, and the animals definitely belong to the same species (which is not always easy to tell with wild-caught specimens), you have the potential for

In nature, female tarantulas (here *Lasiodora parahybana*) aggressively protect their egg cases.

THE GUIDE TO OWNING A TARANTULA

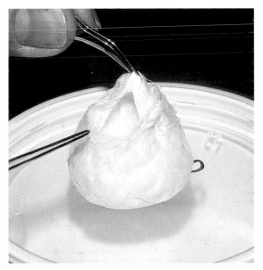
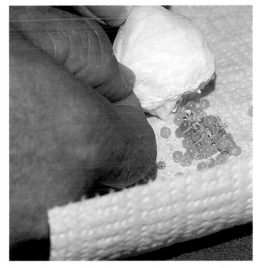

Steps in opening the egg case of *Avicularia avicularia*, the Common Pink-toe, to place the newly hatched spiderlings, embryos, and eggs (below) in a petri dish for further care.

mating. The actions of the male determine when mating will occur. First he has to build a sperm web and capture a few drops of sperm in his sperm bulbs. He builds a small web usually hanging obliquely in one corner of his cage and crawls under it to release onto it a few drops of sperm from his genital opening under the abdomen. Next he crawls on top of the web and reaches around or through it with the emboli of the sperm bulbs (which may have been wetted by secretions from the mouth) and pulls the sperm into the bulbs through capillary action. Once the bulbs are charged, he usually tears down the web. This web-building typically occurs at night and seldom is seen, but traces of the web often are visible the next morning, plus the increased activity of the male and his

First instars of tarantulas often differ greatly in shape and color depending on species. **Above:** *Haplopelma lividum*; **below:** *Lasiodora parahybana.*

seeming desperation to find a female are clues that he now is ready. By the way, as a rule he will have to build a new web and recharge the sperm bulbs before each mating.

Mating must occur in the female's terrarium. Because a female tarantula is fully capable of killing and eating a male both before and after mating, the terrarium must be large enough to allow the male to escape to his own corner. If the female's home terrarium is too small, set up a cage at least 18 inches (45 cm) long and nearly as wide and give it the usual deep substrate plus cover in corners as far apart as possible. Let the female establish herself here for at least a week or two. She will produce the usual burrow or tube-web. Add the male to her terrarium carefully, watching the female's reaction. Be ready to remove him if necessary, having at hand a long pair of forceps and a pair of dowels to help keep the spiders apart and get the male back into a carrying jar if things get rough.

A mature female may spin fine silk lines from the mouth of the burrow that allow her to detect when a male is nearby. Assuming the female is ready, the pair will go through a short period of drumming with the front legs and pedipalps on the substrate and sides of the tank, the male slowly approaching the female and touching her pedipalps with his, followed by caressing motions over her front legs and carapace. If the female is ready, she allows the male to lift up her front legs and thus the front of her body, letting him hook his tibial apophyses into her chelicerae. This does two things: it assures that the female cannot attack the male with her fangs, and it exposes her genital area. He then reaches forward and inserts the tips of the sperm bulbs into the spermathecae, passing on the drops of sperm he has stored. Copulation is rapid, sometimes lasting only two or three minutes.

The male then carefully releases the female, who usually just returns to her retreat, allowing the male to scurry back to his corner. In some cases she reacts more violently and tries to grab him, in which case you will have to intervene. Some keepers let the male stay in the female's cage for a week or two to allow

further matings, but this probably is never really safe. If you want further matings between the pair, return the male to the female's terrarium in a few days. In nature matings almost always happen at night, so keep all light levels low.

EGGS

In three to six months, seldom less and sometimes more, the female will spin a dense web that completely covers her. If she molts and leaves this cocoon in a few days, the sperm are lost with the shed skin and you have to start all over. If she fails to leave the cocoon for several days, she probably is laying her eggs. The stored sperm become active as the eggs are moving through the oviducts to the uterus externus, where fertilization occurs just before the eggs are laid. In a few more days she will pull the edges of

Once fully motile, spiderlings (here *Avicularia avicularia*) are raised in individual containers.

Housing spiderlings in deli cups allows many to be kept in a single outer container to more readily control temperature and humidity.

the cocoon together into a large whitish egg sac that also may contain a covering of urticating hairs in American tarantulas. Egg numbers may range from just a hundred or fewer to well over a thousand. The eggs are free in the cocoon, and the female regularly rotates the cocoon and thus the eggs, keeping them from sticking together. The cocoon helps assure the eggs develop at a proper humidity and temperature partially controlled by the mother. American tarantulas usually carry the cocoon about, but many African and Asian species suspend it in a web in the retreat.

Incubation usually takes six to eight weeks, but in tarantulas development is not quite simple. The large white to brown eggs first develop into postembryos, which look like little shriveled spiders sitting on the eggs. They cannot walk. The next molt is into mobile first instars, which are obviously spiderlings but whose abdomens are still large yolk sacs. Hatching usually occurs in the first instars, which start to tear their way out of the sac while the mother helps by tearing the tough outer layer of the sac. In some species another molt, to the second instar, which is even more spider-like and mobile, occurs before hatching. First instars usually are under a quarter inch (7 mm) long and may be translucent pink with black abdomens but few hairs. When fed on the tiniest crickets and fruitflies, they molt often but still grow slowly, often not reaching an inch (2.5 cm) in length for over a year. Unfortunately, the spiderlings are highly cannibalistic and will feed on each other if given the chance, so after the molt into the second instar, when the yolk sac is used up, they must be separated into individual containers.

TECHNIQUE

Few breeders trust the mother spider to take care of her egg sac because she may destroy it if disturbed too greatly and may eat the spiderlings as soon as they hatch. Usually the egg sac is removed from the mother's care after a month, when most of the eggs may be developed into postembryos. Techniques differ, but often the egg sac is then carefully opened and the postembryos and remaining developing eggs are poured out onto a petri dish with a layer of dry absorbent paper in the bottom. The clutch is separated into manageable groups in different dishes and the whole group is placed in a small plastic box lined with damp paper and held at about 75F (24C); the box is covered to help keep the humidity at 70 to 80%. In two weeks most or all of the eggs will have developed into a mixture of postembryos and first or second instars. As the spiderlings molt into second instars, they are individually removed to small capped vials half-filled with moist vermiculite and peat moss; the caps are pierced with fine holes to allow some air circulation. The humidity in the substrate must be monitored, with water added each week. Feed each spiderling one or two pinhead crickets every other day at first. As the spiderling grows, it will have to be moved to larger containers and

Juvenile tarantulas can be kept in many types of containers, which can lead to quite a bit of clutter. Remember, each one has to be raised separately to avoid cannibalism.

fed larger food. Be sure that crickets are not left unmonitored with molting spiderlings—even tiny crickets can severely damage a soft spiderling. (Fruitflies may establish cultures in spiderling vials, their larve becoming nuisances. They also have been accused of spreading mites to spiderlings.)

PROBLEMS

Learning the proper humidity and container size for each species you breed requires practice or hints from someone who has bred that species before. You at first can expect to lose many spiderlings, but in some ways that solves another problem: numbers of young.

At the moment there are relatively few hobbyists keeping tarantulas and few dealers who handle large numbers of specimens. One mating of a moderately fecund tarantula may easily produce 100 to 1000 young, most of which will become subadults in about a year in the hands of an experienced breeder. What do you do with 1000 specimens of a species, each demanding individual care and feeding, when the entire world demand for that species may be only a few hundred each year? One successful breeding of a tarantula may be enough to in theory supply every hobbyist in the world, and often tens of thousands of spiderlings of a species may be produced.

Spiderlings may take one to three years to attain their full adult shape and coloration. This Colombian Brown, *Pamphobeteus fortis*, has quite a way to develop.

THE GUIDE TO OWNING A TARANTULA

A juvenile *Theraphosa blondi*, the Goliath Bird Eater, is not nearly as impressive as an adult. This is one reason spiderlings are so inexpensive to purchase.

This is why spiderlings often are very inexpensive (plus the fact that they seldom resemble the adult and always look rather plain) until over an inch (2.5 cm) long. Labor costs are tremendous when having to care for individual vials of specimens each week, but the market just will not allow expensive spiderlings of any but the rarest species to be sold. After one successful hatching, even the rarest species in captivity may become common.

This unfortunately spurs a constant search for rarities by commercial collectors and an unending desire to obtain rare species by advanced collectors. Once a species has been bred a few times in captivity, it often is of little interest to advanced tarantula keepers, unfortunately. This really is a matter of supply and demand in a commercial market where a drive to own the unusual determines how the hobby develops.

Poecilotheria fasciata, the Sri Lankan Ornamental, is one of the most brightly patterned tarantulas, but its bite is more dangerous than most.

THE GUIDE TO OWNING A TARANTULA

Familiar Tarantulas

HAIR KICKERS

Though the taxonomy of tarantulas is complex and confused, I think it can be truthfully said that the most familiar hobby tarantulas have come from the American genera *Aphonopelma* and *Brachypelma*. Though most are relatively docile tarantulas—as such things go—and have an innocuous though sometimes temporarily painful bite, they are famous for having developed "hair kicking" into a fine art.

The top of the abdomen of most American tarantulas is home to a variety of different sensory and cosmetic hairs, some of which impart distinctive color patterns to the spider. Important in these tarantulas are urticating (irritating) hairs. These are short, densely packed crystalline hairs most prominent on the upper center of the abdomen. They are loosely set into a base and thus easily dislodged. Instead of a simple hair shaft, they are ornamented with raised spirals that end in small barbs. A hair under strong magnification looks like a repeated series of small fishing hooks. When a *Brachypelma* tarantula, for instance, is disturbed, it holds its ground and turns around, abdomen facing the threat. The hind legs are then raised and rapidly passed over the abdomen, breaking off the urticating hairs and sending them flying toward the attacker like a sea of

A captive-bred Mexican Red-knee, *Brachypelma smithi.*

minute arrows. The hairs rapidly lodge in the soft membranes of the face, especially the nose, throat, and eyes, and instantly cause a burning sensation and local swelling. The hairs can work their way further into the skin and membranes, causing more swelling and irritation as they go. If enough end up in the throat they can cause constriction of the throat; in the eye, they can cause temporary blindness in a small rodent and cataract-like opacity (temporary) in a human. Even when penetrating the tougher skin of the hand and arm, they can cause redness and an annoying itch that may take days to go away.

Additionally, in humans subject to various allergies and asthma attacks the hairs can be dangerous because they stay in the air and are numerous in the spider's webs, so just breathing in the air in and near the cage may cause an allergic reaction of minor to severe intensity.

CARE OF HAIR KICKERS

Though many *Aphonopelma* and *Brachypelma* species are dryland tarantulas, they all are burrowers or at least spend the daylight hours hidden under rocks, logs, or in old rodent burrows. These microhabitats hold much more moisture than the surface air, and to survive the tarantulas need a constant humidity of between 60 and 70% for most species. This is easily supplied in the home in the usual cage with a vermiculite or equivalent substrate, so these spiders are generally considered easy to keep and

good choices for the beginner. They feed readily on crickets, flies, grasshoppers, and other foods appropriate for their size. Captive-bred spiderlings are readily available, often very cheaply, for almost all popular species, though the entire genus *Brachypelma* receives protection under CITES Appendix II, requiring proper permits for both exportation and importation. The most interesting species come from Mexico, which seldom allows legal exportations.

Though nervous, few of these spiders are aggressive attackers, and some have been considered easy to handle—which is not suggested, both for your safety and that of the tarantula. All will bite, however, if provoked or even if just in a bad mood, so never overestimate just how "friendly" or placid they can be. Also remember the problem of the urticating hairs, which may make it impossible for some people with allergies to keep these spiders.

Males tend to mature when about two years old, females maturing when three to five years old. Mating usually is not

***Brachypelma albopilosum*, the Curly Hair Tarantula.**

Brachypelma boehmei, the Flame-leg Tarantula, is one of the most striking additions to the hobby in recent years.

especially aggressive, and females seldom eat their males, but accidents do happen, so be prepared just in case. Females produce the usual large egg sacs that hold between 400 and 700 eggs on average, often more. Hatching may be relatively slow at the usual 75F (24C), sometimes taking ten or more weeks. Spiderlings grow slowly.

Once wild-collected *Brachypelma* were easy to find, but today you will be pleased to purchase 1-inch (2.5-cm) spiderlings at reasonable prices. These juveniles will already be adapted to common terrarium foods and will not be carrying parasites; they also may be used to seeing human hands and faces intruding into their space. The more dully colored *Aphonopelma* species still are wild-collected in the western U.S., but the more colorful forms are captive-bred in fair numbers. Because of the limited market for the brown *Aphonopelma* species, which make excellent, long-lived pets in many cases, one hobby breeding may be enough to supply hobby interest for years.

BRACHYPELMA

There really is no way for a hobbyist to distinguish the genus *Brachypelma* from other similar tarantulas, so most hobbyists just learn to recognize the more colorful species. Technically *Brachypelma* and *Aphonopelma* are very similar, differing mostly in the shorter tip (embolus) of the palpal bulb and presence of feathery (plumose) hairs on the trochanter and femur of the first leg in *Brachypelma* versus a generally longer, more slender and pointed embolus in

Painted Red-legs, *Brachypelma emilia*, come from colonies in western Mexico, and thus all in the hobby should be captive-bred.

Aphonopelma, which lacks plumose hairs on the trochanter and femur of the first leg. Both these characters are difficult to see without magnification even in properly preserved specimens. Hobbyists generally distinguish the species by color and pattern.

Curly Hair Tarantula,

Brachypelma albopilosum: This is an exceptional species in that it comes from moist forests from Guatemala to Costa Rica and thus requires a higher humidity (as much as 80%) in its burrow. Hardy and usually easy to handle (though noted for occasional nervousness), it is considered an excellent beginner's species though captive-bred spiderlings are not always easy to find. The legs and abdomen have long white or golden (not red) hairs that are distinctively curled or curved in most specimens. There is no obvious color pattern on the brown carapace or abdomen.

Flame-knee Tarantula,

Brachypelma auratum: In almost every respect this species looks like the Mexican Red-knee, but the patella is actually dark red in this species, not the orange-red of *B. smithi.* It is more nervous and aggressive than the Red-knee, requires a bit more moisture in the burrow, and is not readily available.

Flame-leg Tarantula,

Brachypelma boehmei: Against a black body, this species has dense orange to rusty red, somewhat curly hairs over the abdomen and the patella, tibia, and metatarsus of each leg. The femur is black. There is no strong pattern on the carapace, which is a coppery brown. This species comes from small colonies in southwestern Mexico, specifically the state of Guerrero, and remains expensive. Also called the Mexican Fire-leg.

Painted Red-leg Tarantula,

Brachypelma emilia: In this species the fifth segment of each leg, the tibia (following the knee or patella), is bright red to yellow and there are reddish hairs on the black abdomen. The carapace coloration is distinctive: coppery tan with a large triangle of black widest at the front and tapering out at about the center of the carapace. It comes from colonies in Durango, western Mexico, and adjacent areas, where it occupies moderately moist burrows. Also called the Mexican Red-leg.

Mexican Red-knee Tarantula,

Brachypelma smithi: In this brightly colored species the patella (knee) segment is bright orange and there is a reddish band across the front edge of the

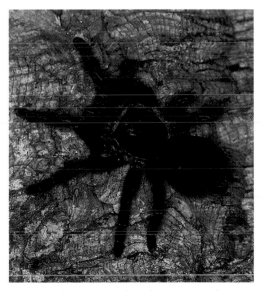

A nice Red-rump, *Brachypelma vagans*; this species now is hard to find.

A young *Brachypelma smithi*, the Mexican Red-knee, with the colors not yet fully developed.

tibia as well. The abdomen is black with scattered pale hairs, while the carapace is glossy black with a broad coppery rim. One of the "classic" tarantulas, it has been protected for 15 years but still is captive-bred in decent numbers and affordable as spiderlings. Coming from western Mexico, it is easy to keep in relatively dry terrariums.

Red-rump Tarantula,

Brachypelma vagans: Once imported in large numbers, today the Red-rump is a moderately expensive captive-bred species. It is basically a black tarantula with grayish outer segments of the legs, a glossy black carapace, and a black abdomen densely covered with very long bright red or orange hairs. Though nervous and sometimes a bit aggressive, it long has been recommended as a beginner's species. It has a wide range in relatively moist habitats (try 70 to 80% humidity) from southern Mexico to at least Panama.

APHONOPELMA

Closely related to *Brachypelma* from more tropical realms, these are the brown tarantulas of the southwestern U.S. and the northern part of Mexico; whether species of this genus occur further into tropical America is uncertain, though a common Costa Rican species usually is placed here. At least a dozen virtually identical shaggy tan to brown or blackish species are found in the U.S. and are easy to collect at night from the spring through autumn, but there is little collector interest in most species.

Mexican Blond Tarantula,

Aphonopelma chalcodes: The tarantula usually sold under this name comes from southeastern Arizona and adjacent Mexico, but its status is uncertain. The carapace is a bright golden tan, while the legs are pale brown and somewhat iridescent; the abdomen is a uniform medium brown. Not an easy species to find as spiderlings, wild-collected adults sometimes are available.

Costa Rican Zebra Tarantula,

Aphonopelma seemanni: One of the least expensive tarantulas to purchase, this species really has little else to attract a hobbyist. It is a species of moist forests in Central America, which should be remembered when setting up its terrarium. It is a uniformly dark brown to black tarantula (the males often darker than the females, though most specimens become dark before molting) with a glossy black carapace and many long grayish hairs on the abdomen and legs. Its

Aphonopelma chalcodes is variously called the Mexican Blond or the Tucson Blond; specimens come from southern Arizona.

THE GUIDE TO OWNING A TARANTULA

The Costa Rican Zebra or Striped-knee, *Aphonopelma seemanni*, needs considerable humidity in its terrarium.

distinctive feature is the presence of a pair of pale stripes on the knee (patella) and tibia; the femur usually is blacker than the rest of the leg. There may be pale rings around the ends of the femur, patella, and tibia, but these are never wide. The front of the carapace is white, and often the edges are pale as well. Though it has been widely suggested as a

Grammostola, the Chilean rose tarantulas, contains several virtually identical species.

replacement for the Mexican Red-knee, it really is too nervous for beginners and is not always easy to keep healthy. It also is called the Striped-knee Tarantula.

SOME SOUTH AMERICAN TERRESTRIALS

There are hundreds of species of tarantulas in the tropics and subtropics of South America, and many of them lately have appeared in the hobby. Most are not distinctive in appearance, are aggressive, and sometimes die suddenly. Few are available as captive-bred spiderlings at affordable prices. The following species (some of uncertain identification) often appear in the shops.

Chilean Common Tarantula, *Grammostola rosea:* Representative of a group of several very similar 3-inch (7.5 cm), relatively hairy-legged species from

Recently *Lasiodora parahybana*, the Brazilian Salmon Pink Tarantula, has been bred in large numbers and become widely available.

dry regions of Chile and adjacent areas, this species once was called *G. spatulata; G. cala* (Chilean Rose) is very similar. Basically a pale to medium brown tarantula, the legs are covered with long pale hairs that are distinctly rusty or

Goliath Bird Eaters, *Theraphosa blondi*, have little to recommend them except size.

pinkish on the femur; the carapace has a strong rosy tinge in many specimens, and there are pale reddish hairs on the abdomen. It does well in a fairly dry terrarium and does even better if allowed to spend two months each year at somewhat drier and cooler conditions than normal. Though it breeds easily in captivity, it often is nervous and aggressive.

Brazilian Salmon Pink Tarantula,

Lasiodora parahybana: This dark brown southern Brazilian spider is one of the largest tarantulas, with a body length of up to 4 inches (10 cm) and a legspan in males of over 9 inches (22.5 cm). The legs

THE GUIDE TO OWNING A TARANTULA

are covered with long pale brown hairs, and the front of the carapace has a wide white fringe of hairs. The femur is black, with only short hairs. Nervous, aggressive, and not a good pet, this species is kept mostly for its large size. One mating may produce over a thousand spiderlings.

Goliath Bird Eater,

Theraphosa blondi: Said to be the largest living tarantula, with a body length of almost 5 inches (12 cm) and a legspan in males of 10 inches (25 cm), this brown, otherwise unremarkable species is found in moist habitats from Venezuela eastward across northern South America. The carapace is almost round in females, while the legs are not as hairy as in the Brazilian Salmon Pink. There may be a pair of pale reddish stripes on the patella. Always in demand and expensive, this tarantula is too aggressive for the casual hobbyist.

SOME AMERICAN TREE TARANTULAS

The subfamily Aviculariinae includes several South American arboreal tarantulas that appear regularly in the hobby both as captive-bred spiderlings and wild-caught adults. These species need tall terrariums, produce many urticating hairs that cover their tube-webs, and may be very aggressive and nervous, escaping readily. The common genus, *Avicularia*, the pink-toes, contains many very similar species. Because of a fear that the spiders could become established in southern Florida (not impossible), sale of these tarantulas is restricted in Florida. (Recently Florida has required a permit for most sales of exotic spiders within the state; expect other areas to follow suit.)

Antillean Pink-toe Tarantula,

Avicularia versicolor: Most pink-toe juveniles have a pattern of broad dark

Though restricted to Martinique, the Antillean Pink-toe, *Avicularia versicolor*, is widely available but remains expensive.

Juvenile Antillean Pink-toes display the banded abdominal pattern typical of the genus.

bands across the abdomen along with a middorsal dark band, and this is true of juveniles of this species. Adults, however, are stunning spiders with iridescent metallic green carapaces and rusty red abdomens. The 2-inch (5 cm) adults are relatively unaggressive and are bred in decent numbers in captivity; it originates in Martinique in the Lesser Antilles north of South America. One of the more popular tarantulas, it remains expensive. The nearly all-black *Avicularia metallica* comes from the Guianas and adjacent Brazil. In both these species and their relatives the tips of the tarsi are bright pink to rusty red (especially in males), the origin of the common name. The species of *Avicularia* need consistently high humidity, preferably 90% or more, or they desiccate in a matter of hours. Though quite keepable, they are far more delicate than terrestrial species.

Trinidad Chevron Tarantula,

Psalmopoeus cambridgei: This large (body length almost 3 inches, 7.5 cm),

This stunning male Antillean Pink-toe has a metallic green carapace and bright red abdomen.

THE GUIDE TO OWNING A TARANTULA

hairy-legged arboreal species comes from Trinidad, the island just north of Venezuela. Though gray to brownish in general tones, it has a bright orange spot or stripe on top of each tarsus and sometimes on the metatarsus. These are very fast, very aggressive spiders that are hard to control and are noted for heavily webbing their cage. This species does not require quite as humid an environment as *Avicularia* species. Though females produce relatively few eggs, captive-bred spiderlings can be found if you look around.

Other arboreal American tarantulas are imported occasionally but seldom are bred in sufficient numbers to reach the commercial market. All arboreal tarantulas tend to be fast and aggressive, as well as demanding high humidity, a relatively large terrarium, and a tolerance for lots of dirty-looking webbing over the cage. They cannot be recommended for beginners, though it would be hard to pass up a cheap Antillean Pink-toe.

FROM THE OLD WORLD: KEEP AWAY!

As more and more American tarantulas have been placed under varying degrees of protection, many strange, often large, and almost always extremely aggressive tarantulas have been imported from tropical Africa and southern Asia. At the moment these are popular with tarantula specialists, but under no circumstances can they be suggested for an inexperienced hobbyist. Additionally, most are quite expensive and not often bred in captivity. At least some or perhaps most have a very venomous bite that

Trinidad Chevrons, *Psalmopoeus cambridgei*, are tree tarantulas that seldom are available. Notice the spot of orange on the tarsus typical of the species.

A juvenile, still colorful, King Baboon, *Citharischius crawshayi.*

could cause hospitalization. Be very careful when feeding, cleaning, or transferring these spiders.

Curved Horn Baboon Tarantula,

Ceratogyrus bechuanicus: The major claim to fame of the species of this genus is the presence of a dark brown tubercle just behind the center of the carapace. In this species the tubercle or horn points backward. This southern African species is about 2 inches (5 cm) in body length, with a slender, rather elongated abdomen that is dark gray or brown, spotted or dappled with pale gray. It can be kept like most terrestrial species and tolerates a humidity as low as 50%, though 60 to 80% is better. It webs extensively and will form a dense, unattractive den area in one corner of the terrarium as well as a shallow burrow. Very aggressive, it

Ceratogyrus brachycephalus (here a female) is one of the several tarantulas bearing a dark knob or "horn" on the carapace. The horned baboons are all from southern Africa.

The starburst baboons are large, aggressive, but interestingly patterned tarantulas of arid southern Africa. This is *Pterinochilus murinus*, the Mombasa Starburst.

Pterinochilus meridionalis, the Zimbabwe Gray or Mustard Baboon, has an interesting dappled abdominal pattern.

An adult female King Baboon, *Citharischius crawshayi*, has enlarged, slightly bowed hind legs and relatively little color.

belongs to a subfamily (Harpactirinae) known to contain dangerously venomous species.

King Baboon Tarantula,

Citharischius crawshayi: Currently this large (often over 3 inches, 7.5 cm, body length) and exceedingly aggressive tarantula from dry sections of southeastern Africa is quite popular though certainly not a simple species to keep. Females, the sex usually seen, have very large, bowed hind legs with which they dig burrows over 6 feet (1.8 meters) deep. This means that in the terrarium it needs a substrate at least 8 to 12 inches (20 to 30 cm) deep to be comfortable.

Though a dangerous biter, it is attractive and distinctive in its coat of short reddish brown hairs over the abdomen and the faint black starburst on the carapace. When it lifts the front legs to show the large fangs (which is often and repeatedly at any movement), patches of red and black hairs become visible. Dangerous, fast, and not commonly bred in captivity, it is not for the casual tarantula keeper.

Ornamental Tarantulas,

Poecilotheria spp.: Once major rarities in the terrarium, the brightly patterned species of *Poecilotheria* from India and Sri Lanka now are fairly popular with specialists, several species being present

THE GUIDE TO OWNING A TARANTULA

The bright yellow bands under the front legs of the Sri Lankan Ornamental Tarantula, *Poecilotheria fasciata*, are exposed when the cornered spider rears back in defense.

Still imported from Sri Lanka but now also captive-bred, the Sri Lankan Ornamental Tarantula has become popular but is too dangerous for beginners.

in the hobby. They tend to be grayish and may have elaborate gray, black, and brown patterns on the carapace and abdomen, along with narrow yellowish to orange stripes and bands on the legs. When they lift the front part of the body in defense, most species display brilliant colors, often red at the bases of the chelicerae and yellow, gray, and red bands under the pedipalps and front two pairs of legs. Males and females may have somewhat different coloration. In nature the ornamental tarantulas live in treeholes, so they need a very tall (16 to 20 inches, 40 to 50 cm) terrarium with snags with predug holes or even small bird houses. They can be kept colonially if each specimen is given its own house, but this requires a large display terrarium. Adults tend to be 2 to 3 inches (5 to 7.5 cm) in body length, with long legs; the abdomen is long and cylindrical as in most Old World tarantulas. At least some species of this genus can produce a dangerously venomous bite, they are fast, and they are nervous, so great care is advised if you try to keep one. Spiderlings are very expensive at the moment.

Leopard Palm Tarantula,
Stromatopelma calceatum: Coming from tropical savannas of western Africa, this species may be common on palm trees near villages. This is a 2.5-inch (6-cm) arboreal tarantula that somewhat resembles *Poecilotheria* in pattern, being grayish with a rather elaborate dark pattern on the carapace and abdomen and often with rings and spots on the very hairy legs. They lack the bright colors under the legs, however. Palm or featherleg tarantulas can be kept at 70 to 80% humidity in a tall terrarium. This is a

Stromatopelma calceatum, often called the Featherleg, is known to have a dangerous bite and also is highly aggressive. It cannot be recommended for any but specialists.

The large West African species of *Hysterocrates* seldom are seen but have attractive patterns. However, they should be approached with caution and are not good for beginners.

very aggressive species noted for standing its ground when challenged and actually attacking on occasion. The venom is reported to cause an irregular heart beat that may begin long after the original bite; hospitalization may be required.

Though this is just a very small sampling of the Old World tarantulas, it is not misleading. Currently the newest, rarest imports from southern Asia tend to be large, extremely aggressive, and often not identifiable to genus or species, a very disturbing situation when dealing with animals with potentially very dangerous venom.

THE FUTURE

Are tarantulas here to stay as terrarium pets? Probably, though it would not take more than one or two serious, highly publicized accidents to cause laws to be enacted prohibiting their sale. Already they are classified as dangerous animals under some regional and local laws, and they may require permits for legal sale or keeping. The future definitely lies in making suitably attractive, relatively docile species available cheaply as captive-bred spiderlings, but unfortunately this may not happen. A recent dealer listing offered more than 40 species of captive-bred tarantulas for sale at low to very high prices, but over half would be considered brownish look-alikes by casual hobbyists. Some hobbyists currently tend to collect the largest, most aggressive species as some type of show of bravado, behavior that is sure to lead to trouble in the future.

Whether tarantulas will continue to be freely available depends on you. If you stick to captive-bred species that are relatively easy to keep and unlikely to cause bad press for the hobby, and especially if they are colorful to boot, we may have a future.

Resources

FURTHER READING

Charpentier, Phillip. nd (1994?).
"The genus *Avicularia*," *Exothermae,* 1(1): not paginated.

Charpentier, Phillip. nd (1996?).
"Les mechanismes de defense des mygales," *Exothermae Magazine,* #0: not paginated.

DeVosjoli, Philippe. 1991.
Arachnomania. Advanced Vivarium Systems, Lakeside, CA.

Foeliz, Rainer F. 1996.
Biology of Spiders. Oxford Univ. Press, NY.

Gurley, Russ. 1993.
A Color Guide to Tarantulas of the World I. Russ Gurley, Ada, OK.

Gurley, Russ. 1995.
A Color Guide to Tarantulas of the World II. Russ Gurley, Ada, OK.

Kaston, B. J. 1972 (and later editions).
How to Know the Spiders. Wm. C. Brown Co., Dubuque, Iowa.

Moore, Mary Edith. 1998.
"Raising tarantula spiderlings," *Reptile Hobbyist,* 4(3): 83-87.

Smith, Andrew N. 1994.
A Study of the Theraphosidae Family from North America. Fitzgerald Publ., London.

Tinter, Andreas. 1996.
Tarantulas Today. T.F.H. Publ., Neptune City, NJ.

Verdez, J. M., F. Cleton & P. Gerard. 1997.
L'elevage des Mygales. Paris.

SOCIETIES

American Tarantula Society
P.O. Box 756
Carlsbad, New Mexico 88221
http://atshq.org/

British Tarantula Society
C/o Mrs. Ann Webb
81 Phillimore Place
Radlett, Hertfordshire
WD7 8NJ United Kingdom
http://www.bts.ndirect.co.uk

Index

Page numbers in **bold** indicate photographs

Photo Credits

R. D. Bartlett: p. 5; 23; 27; 33; 48; 51 top
Paul Freed: p. 3 (Chromatopelma cyaneopubescens); 24; 56 top; 57 top
James E. Gerholdt: p. 7; 17; 18; 20; 22; 25; 42; 43; 44; 46; 47; 52 top; 53; 57 bottom; 58
Michael Gilroy: p. 49 bottom
Erik Loza: p. 14; 16; 19; 32; 55; 61
Barry Mansell: p. 9
Gerold & Cindy Merker: p. 4; 13; 45; 50; 59 bottom
Gerald L. Moore: 34; 35; 37 all; 38 both; 39; 40; 41; 54 both
Mark Smith: p. 6; 49 top; 51 bottom; 59 top; 60
Stan Sung: p. 15
Karl H. Switak: p. 1 (Brachypelma smithi); 36; 52 bottom; 56 bottom
John C. Tyson: p. 11; 21